WOLVES
UNLEASHED

WOLVES
UNLEASHED

Andrew Simpson

RMB
Victoria Vancouver Calgary

Contents

Introduction

Growing up in Scotland in an isolated area with only a few scattered houses, where the nearest town had less than 200 people, I never imagined I would end up travelling the world training animals for the film industry.

As a boy I was always fascinated by nature. From collecting tadpoles to finding an old bird's nest, everything seemed unique to me in its own way. One of my junior-school report cards points out that "… Andrew's attention seems to focus on anything that moves, crawls or flies …"

Our family always had at least one dog in the house. Once my brother Norman and I were old enough to have our own dog, the adventures began to happen. Scamp was our best friend, playing soccer, climbing up mountains and waiting for us after school. He was always there and stayed with my parents long after my brother and I had left home, until he died at age 18.

One day Norman and I were working outdoors on a snowy wet winter's day. The night before, we had gone to see the Mel Gibson film *The Road Warrior*, which was set in Australia. During lunch, as we complained about the weather, Norman suggested I should go and see Australia, since it looked so great in the film. A few months later I left for the great land Down Under on an adventure that would change my life forever. I was 20 years old.

Back in the early eighties things were different. You could still board a plane with a knife in your pocket and it was relatively safe to travel around Australia with just a pack thrown over your shoulder, which I spent several months doing. During one of those months I came across a film being made close to Ayers Rock called *A Cry in the Dark*, which was based on a true story about a young baby being stolen from a couple's tent by a wild dingo. I managed to get a job as an extra going up and down Ayers Rock several times a day, and during my spare time I would watch the filming. I was intrigued by the way the trainer got the dingos to work in front of the camera. It was my first introduction to the use of animals in the film industry.

During the next few years, I travelled between Scotland, Australia, New Zealand and Canada. Every now and then I would get lucky and find a film production to work on. But it wasn't until another trip to Australia that I got a chance to work with animals in a film. The movie was called *Quigley Down Under*, with Tom Selleck. And once more they had working dingos and also some kangaroos. I started off as an extra again before asking if I could work with the animals. After spending a few days with the dingos and holding kangaroos by the tail, I was hooked.

Before I moved to Canada in the early nineties my last job was on *Braveheart*, with Mel Gibson. It was funny to me that the actor in the film that originally inspired me to leave home was now in my home country filming and I was leaving!

It wasn't until I moved to Canada that I got fully involved in the movie industry. My job every day was working with dogs, cats, birds, deer, rats, bears and wolves – basically any animals you would ever see on television or in a film. Whether it's a rat in a sewer or a bird on a gatepost, they are all animal actors, owned and trained by someone.

When I look back on my early years working with animals, I realize I was blessed to work with so many different ones. Every species you handle teaches you a little more and in turn makes you a better trainer because you have to adapt and change your style each time. What works with one bear may not work

with another, so you are in a constant learning pattern, trying to understand what makes them tick. Many of the animal companies today try to keep a wide selection of everything, because they never know, when the phone rings, what will be needed. It could be a dog, a tiger, maybe even a crow. So they have many different species on hand at any given time.

I made the choice to specialize in just one species: the wolf. This way I could devote my time and energy to making them the best they could be. In my opinion, wolves are one of the hardest animals to work on a film set. They are fully aware of everything around them and they are constantly assessing every situation presented to them. This behaviour is in their nature. It's their instinct. It's how they have managed to survive and adapt for thousands of years. And although our wolves are bred and raised in captivity, the wild instinct is never far beneath the surface.

Normally when you get a telephone call asking for a wolf to be used in a film, it's usually for a day or two, or if you are lucky maybe a couple of weeks. When I got the call about working on the French production of *Loup*, though, it was quite different. The film in English was going to be called Wolf and it was going to be about wolves, and it was going to feature wolves. But it was going to be filmed in Siberia!

Once I got over my initial shock at the location, I started to get excited about the possibility of actually working on this project. I firmly believe life is for taking chances and going outside your comfort zone. And this was about as far outside as you could go.

Having read the script and taken the job, I got down to sorting out the logistics. Taking wolves to Russia is not an easy task, especially since no one had ever done it before. We had no reference to help us out. The paperwork to get the wolves into Russia from Canada had to be designed from scratch and translated into both Russian and the two Canadian official languages. The forms were sent back and forth many times before everyone could agree on a final version. Once the paperwork was done, we started on the blood testing, vaccinations and various other necessities for both wolves and trainers before we could travel. Altogether it took six months to complete all the requirements.

Travelling to Siberia was its own separate adventure, a sort of cross between reality tv and a game show. Anything that could happen did and usually several times a day, it seemed. The kicker for us was that we not only endured this trip in the dead of winter but then had to repeat it in the swelter of summer. It felt like Siberia could be just as brutal in any season.

Much of the action the script required of the wolves had never been done before or even attempted before. And to be totally honest I was not sure if we could successfully do it. We would be putting wolves in unnatural situations with their natural prey and asking them to just forget all their instincts and listen to us. Touching on the edge of crazy there, maybe?

Despite everything we went through during the filming, though, I am glad we took the chance and experienced it all. It not only gave me a new perspective on many things, but also allowed me to make my documentary *Wolves Unleashed*, along with this companion book.

The wolf truly is one of the most misunderstood animals of all time. For centuries they have been hunted, poisoned, trapped and persecuted in ways that make no sense to me. My biggest hope is that people will watch the film and read this book and take away a different view of the wolf. I hope people can see an animal that is trusting, intelligent, caring, funny, affectionate and the farthest thing from the evil beast so many people perceive to be.

Acknowledgements

Sometimes it's not until you have to sit down and write about the people you wish to thank that you realize just how many people are important to you. For me it's not just the people who helped with this book but also those who have helped me in my life and have made an impression on it. For without these people and the experiences we have shared I would not be the person I am today.

My parents had a huge positive effect on my life. They never held me back. They encouraged my wandering around the world in search of adventure, and they were always supportive and proud to tell my story to anyone who would listen. My father, Norman Simpson, died far too early. His passing left a hole in our family that is still there today, but the influence he had on me is ever-present in everything I do. Shona Simpson, my mother, is a solid rock for everyone, including me. She is the most caring, loving mother anyone could ever have. If there were more people like her in the world, it would be a better place. I would like to use these lines to let her know I am proud of her and the strength she has shown since the passing of my father.

Equally important to me is the close bond I have with my brother, Norman J. Simpson. Despite our having taken different paths in our lives and living many miles apart, he has always had my back whenever I have needed him and I hope one day to repay that.

I would also like to thank Angus McDonald, my uncle and role model during the most important years in my life. Kerry Hummel, thank you for taking me under your wing when I first arrived in Canada. Ruth LaBarge, thank you for being there as my friend when I needed one the most. To Kim and David Canham, thank you for welcoming me into your home and letting me be part of your life. Tina Sarantis, thank you for getting inside my head and making my thoughts into something great. Todd Bulmiller, thank you for your endless hours helping me make an award-winning film. And to Don Gorman and RMB, thank you for taking a chance and for giving me a chance.

Never, while growing up, did I expect wolves would become such a big part of my life. I could never have imagined waking up every day to the sound of 22 wolves howling outside my house, but I would not change the way things have turned out for me. The wolves featured in the film and in this book mean the world to me. I have given up many things in my life for them, as they have given up for me. Each one will stay with me until their last moments on this earth; they will not be abandoned or forgotten. I hope both the film and this book will help to change people's understanding about wolves and show the true nature of these wonderful animals.

Although my team are featured in this book, it's a shame that photos cannot show spirit and personality. Each member is so different from all the others, but put them all together, especially in an extreme situation such as we experienced, and they all pull together and become an unbreakable group. Despite the harsh conditions we faced every day, we always found time to laugh about something. And that is the glue that held us together. I could not have done this without them.

Photos can capture moments in time that might otherwise be forgotten. The majority of the images in this book I owe to my oldest friend, David Gilchrist. Without his constant frozen fingers on a camera, many moments that would have gone unseen by anyone outside of the film crew. And I would also like to thank the crew members of *Loup* for swapping photos with me in exchange for posing with their favorite wolf when filming ended. Many of their photos are featured in this book. I tried really hard to get all the credits correct, but if I made any mistakes it was not intentional and I apologize.

The last acknowledgement I would like to make is to Sally Jo. Over the last few years, she has brought happiness, laughter and love into my life in ways I never knew existed. She has made my house a home and she has followed me around the world several times as I pursued my dreams and goals. Despite all the frozen places I have taken her to and all the lonely nights she spent by herself when I was locked in an office somewhere trying to make a film and write a book, there were no complaints from her, only bright smiles. She has inspired me to be a better person. She has taught me that life is for living and shown me what is important. Her endless love and kindness to my wolves and her many sleepless nights raising them beside me are priceless. Sally, I love you.

Both the winter and the summer trips had their own problems for us. Even today when I look at the photos or watch the film, I can remember every step of the journey getting to the Siberian location.

I knew where the wolf camp was going to be located because I had been there on a scouting trip a few months earlier. But getting there by myself was a whole lot easier than travelling with a pack of wolves.

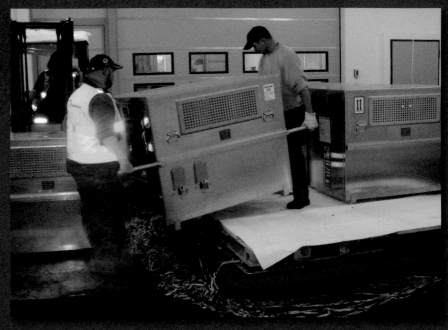

Our journey began in Canada, then to Frankfurt, Germany. Next was a cargo plane to Krasnoyarsk, Russia, where we once again switched planes to fly to Yakutsk.

Once we finally arrived in Yakutsk and spent several hours clearing paperwork with the Customs office, it was time to load the wolves into the travel truck.

During this whole trip I stayed with the wolves. In three different planes, three different countries, freezing trucks and empty warehouses, we experienced everything together. They were my responsibility and I would not leave them alone.

SPEED WAS A FACTOR IN SUMMER TRAVEL DUE TO THE FACT WE HAD SUCH YOUNG PUPS WITH US THIS TIME. SO WE USED A PRIVATE JET TO FLY US FROM CANADA OVER ALASKA AND INTO YAKUTSK.

When we arrived in Yakutsk, the heat was unbearable; the only shade available to us while we waited for Customs clearance was under the plane's wing.

Once we left Yakutsk the adventure had just begun.
We were faced with breakdowns, unscheduled ferries and
ripped-up bridges.

ONCE AGAIN I TRAVELLED WITH THE WOLVES. I WOULD EAT AND SLEEP HERE WITH THEM AS WE TRAVELLED TO THE CAMP. THE BACK OF THE TRUCK BECAME MY "THINK TANK" AS I SPENT MY TIME GOING OVER NOTES AND SCRIPT SCENARIOS IN MY HEAD.

EVERY SO OFTEN WE WOULD STOP TO GIVE OURSELVES AND THE
WOLVES A CHANCE TO STRETCH OUR LEGS AND TAKE A BREAK FROM

It was impossible to show everything about the journey we did or to fully explain it to people when they ask. For us, it was just a blur of days and events that all blended together. But I hope the pictures I have chosen will give you a sense of what we all went through.

I have been asked many times if I would do it all again, and if I'm being honest, I would have to say no.

This was one of the first scenes we shot with the wolves. It was so cold and it hurt just to be there. Every part of your body felt like it could break off at any second! It was the first time the young actor and Digger would meet in front of the camera. And there was no doubt in my mind that they were both as cold as I was.

BEFORE ANY FILMING TOOK PLACE BETWEEN DIGGER
AND THE ACTOR, NICOLAS BRIOUDES, INTRODUCTIONS
NEEDED TO BE MADE. AS WAS OFTEN THE CASE, THE
ACTOR SHOWED A TREMENDOUS AMOUNT OF COURAGE IN
DEALING WITH AN ADULT WOLF. BECAUSE THIS WAS NOT
SOMETHING NORMAL PEOPLE DO EVERY DAY. DURING ALL
OF THESE EXERCISES THE WOLVES' FOCUS IS KEPT ON ME.

WE FIRST LET THEM BOTH STAND SIDE BY SIDE SO
THEY CAN BE TOGETHER WITHOUT ANY PRESSURE TO
INTERACT. THEN WE ASK THE ACTOR TO KNEEL BESIDE
THE WOLF. THIS LETS THEM BOTH FEEL EACH OTHER'S
ENERGY IN A SAFE, CONTROLLED SITUATION. ONCE THE
ACTOR IS COMFORTABLE BEING BESIDE THE WOLF IT'S
TIME FOR A FACE-TO-FACE MEETING.

The final step is to have Digger lie down on the actor, this is the true test to see if they are both comfortable working with each other. Now we have taken the first steps in creating the "magical bond" required for the film.

WHEN PEOPLE WATCH THE FINISHED
FILM AND SEE THESE INTIMATE
MOMENTS BETWEEN AN ACTOR AND
A WOLF CAPTURED ON FILM, THEY
MAY NEVER REALIZE THE IMMENSE
PRESSURE AND FOCUS ON BOTH THE
TRAINER AND THE WOLF THAT IS EVER

THE LOCALS USE REINDEER FOR EVERYTHING FROM FOOD TO CLOTHING TO TRANSPORT. OUR TWO BIGGEST CHALLENGES ON THIS PROJECT WAS THE FACT THE WOLVES WOULD BE WORKING FREE WITH THE REINDEER, WHICH ARE A NATURAL PREY FOR THEM. AND THAT THE ACTOR WAS GOING TO BE WEARING "HEAD TO TOE" REAL FUR AND HIDE CLOTHING, WHICH WE REFERRED TO AS THE "FUR SUIT OF TEMPTATION" FOR THE WOLVES.

Once we had spent some time getting the wolves familiar with the fur suit, we had a corral built next to our wolf area so the wolves could begin to get used to the sight and smells of the reindeer. After that, whenever we could, we would walk the wolves over to meet the reindeer without fences between them.

Surprisingly the wolves would show little interest in the deer unless they began to move quickly. Then the hunting instinct kicked into gear — a major hurdle when dealing with a predator and prey combination.

Sometimes the wolves' hunting instinct helped us get the shots required. By teaching the wolves to focus on and chase a fur lure, we could simulate scenes like the wolves breaking into the corral without them even thinking about the reindeer inside.

The wolves had to learn which fur things were ok to bite and which ones were not. They would spend one day chasing and getting to rip apart a fur lure for fun, then the next day they would have to work within inches of the actor and totally ignore the suit he was wearing and the reindeer around them.

By letting the wolves have fun with the lure and making it a game they always won, it allowed them to get any instinctual desire or frustration out of their systems. They could then focus on work when required and ignore the temptations around them.

Once you got over the shock of discovering there was no running water and no showers, the experience of the banja was something you began to look forward to at the end of the day. The system was quite ingenious, made from rough-cut lumber with moss packed in between the wood for insulation. The whole thing took on a Scandinavian feel. The entrance was where you undressed and also where you fed the fire for the main hot water tank. This was a crude but effective system consisting of a fire box with a water tank on top that you filled manually with water or blocks of ice.

This tank went through the wall into the second room, where you bathed. On this side you had a tap connected to the hot water tank. Next to that was a barrel of ice-cold water taken from the frozen lake.

The idea is you mix hot and cold water in the red basins provided and then use the large ladle to pour the water onto yourself. From getting clean at the end of the day, to weekend laundry, it was a great system for the middle of the mountains.

THE MOST COMMON SIGHTS IN THE CAMP IN WINTER WERE PILES OF FROZEN WOLF CHICKEN, PILES OF FROZEN FIREWOOD, PILES OF FROZEN ICE AND THE ODD FROZEN FISH FOR DINNER. AND OF COURSE, THE CAMP STRAY, POUBELLE, WHO SUCCEEDED IN WINNING A PLACE IN OUR HEARTS.

When you see the summer aerial photo of the camp you see just how beautiful and remote this location is. One of my first experiences on this project was standing looking at a half-finished framework of a building in Yakutsk and being told we would live in these all winter. At the time, I was thinking "you can't be serious." I never imagined at that moment that they would turn out as nice and as comfortable as they did. A remarkable achievement by the Russian construction team.

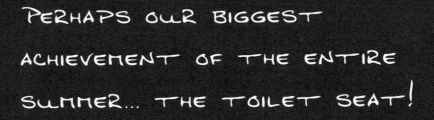

PERHAPS OUR BIGGEST ACHIEVEMENT OF THE ENTIRE SUMMER... THE TOILET SEAT!

Without question, the day Digger fell into the ice hole was one of my hardest days on a film set.

To walk on thin ice was not something we could train the wolf to do — they are too smart for that. But when Digger began walking, he kept his focus on me as if he believed the ice would hold him because I was there.

The safest way to control this sequence was to make a hole in a frozen river. The local crew used chainsaws and ice picks to cut their way to the bottom of the river. Water was brought to the location to fill the hole, which was then covered in powdered snow and left to freeze.

When Digger fell through the ice, it was a shock to him and he looked at me in disbelief. Even the fact I knew he was 100 per cent safe, I felt gutted. I had betrayed his trust – trust that had taken so long to earn.

Normally at the end of the filming day, you leave feeling good about your day's work, but that day I didn't. That day was hard – not physically hard, but emotionally hard. Somehow I felt I had let us both down.

For the next three nights, Digger slept in my room. The room next door was occupied by the film's producer. He made a passing comment that he could smell the wet wolf. But I was ok with that — it was the least I could do to try and rebuild the relationship with Digger.

Dragged Behind the Sled

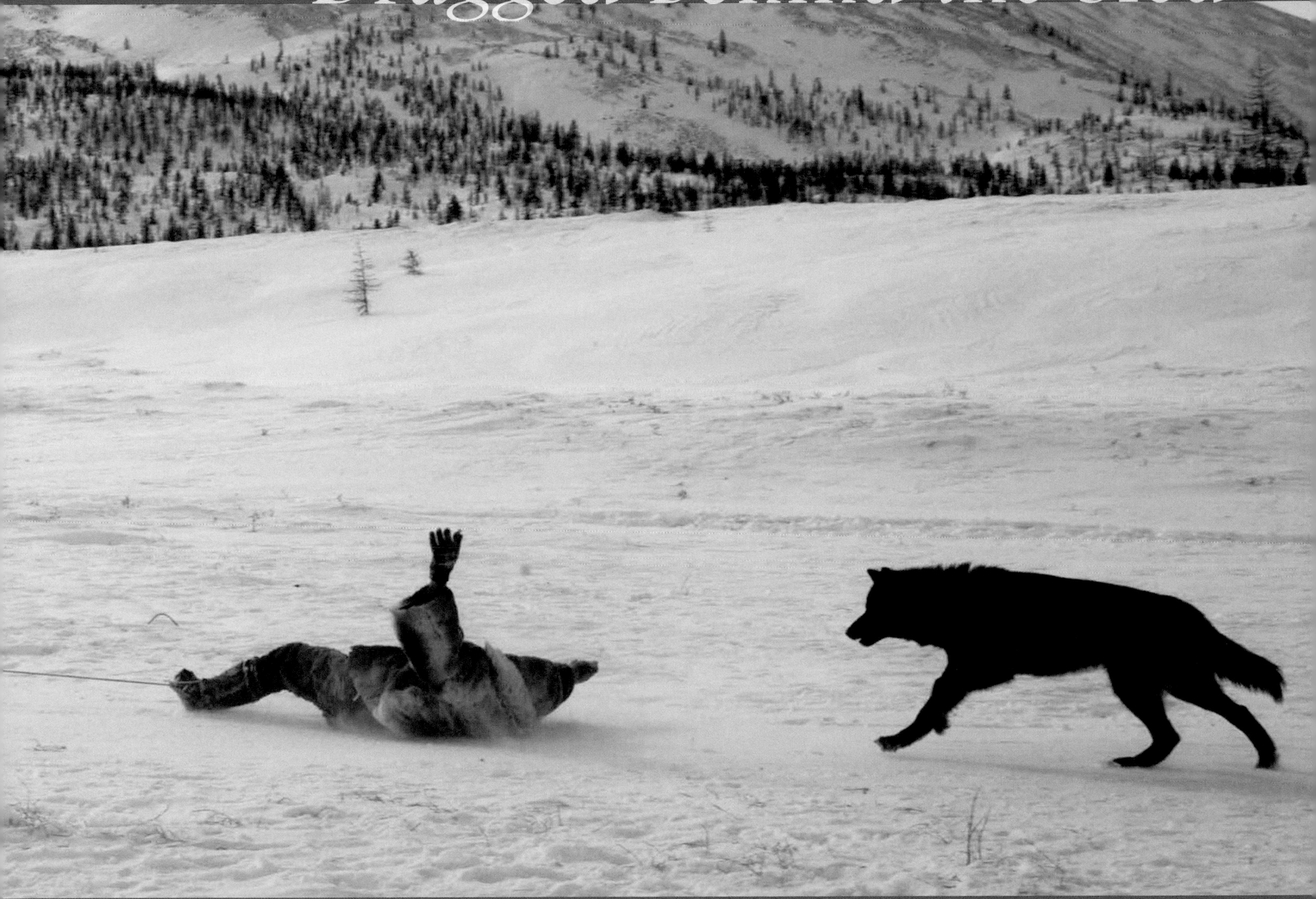

This was one of these things you agree to do while sitting around a table during a production meeting. It always seems easy in the warmth of a heated room when the creative juices are flowing ...

THE PLAN WAS SIMPLE. DRESS ME LIKE THE ACTOR, TIE A ROPE AROUND MY LEG, CONNECT THE ROPE TO A SLED BEING PULLED BY TWO REINDEER AND HAVE A WOLF CHASE ME AND BITE MY ARM!

FOR BOTH WOLVES, TYKA AND 2-TOES, THIS WAS JUST FUN. IT WAS VERY SIMILAR TO THEM CHASING THE HOMEMADE REINDEER LURE WE HAD SHOWN THEM EARLIER IN THEIR TRAINING.

After we had done this several times and everybody was happy, I'd like to say I felt ok. But the truth was my leg felt just as you would expect it to feel after being dragged behind a sled. It hurt like hell!

During our travels on the roads in Siberia, we were constantly amazed by the size and types of trucks we saw and the loads they would carry. Some of them would fit right into a Hollywood apocalyptic film without any trouble.

DESPITE THE SIZE AND TOUGH APPEARANCE OF THESE VEHICLES, THE DANGERS OF THE WINDING MOUNTAIN ROADS WERE EVER PRESENT.

Running Free

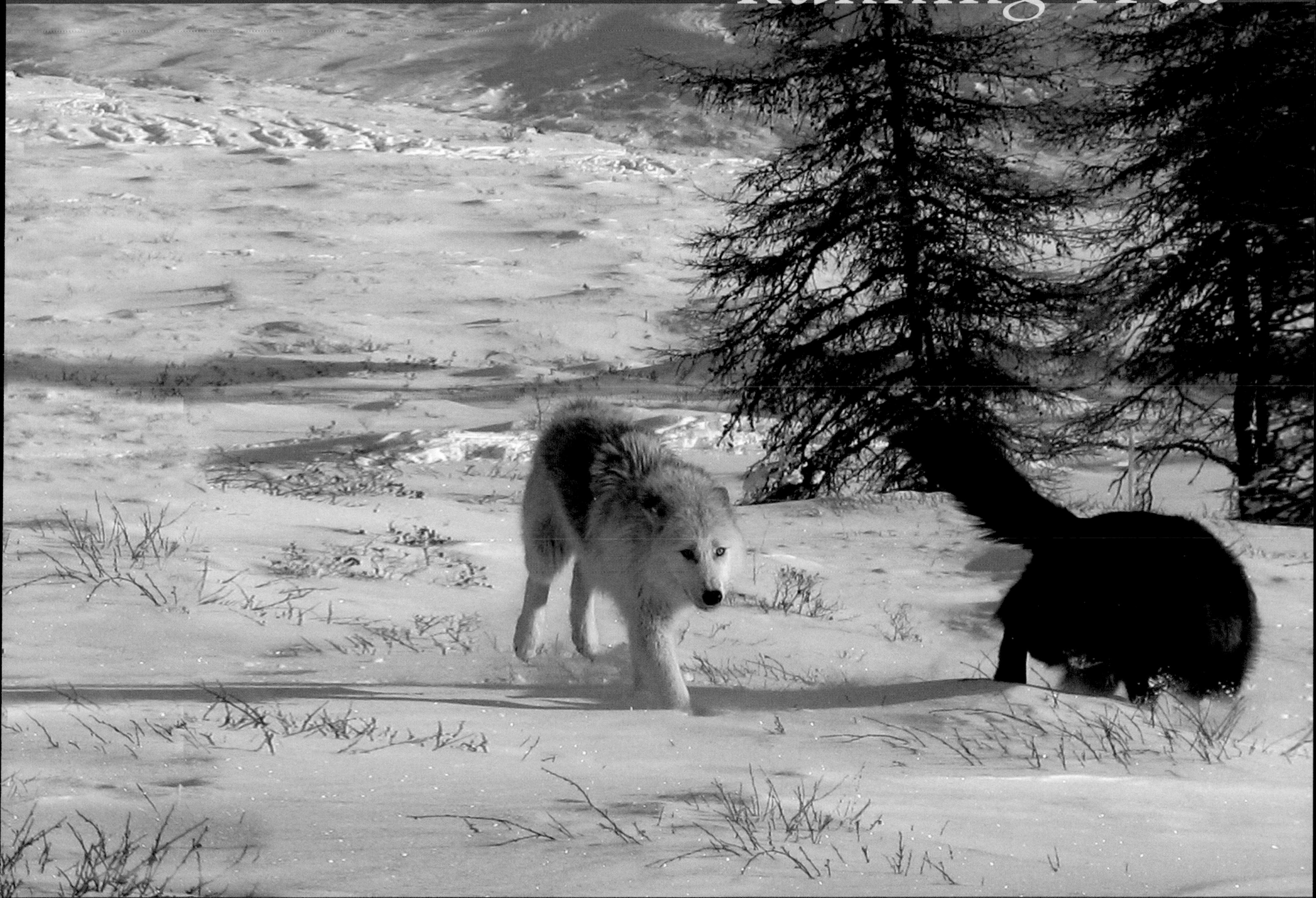

Whenever we would let the wolves run together, they seemed to have an endless supply of energy. They covered great distances effortlessly while chasing each other and playing in the snow. It was pure fun for them and I swear that in some of the photos, you can see them smiling.

Sometimes we would place trainers in different areas and call the wolves to us in random directions. This gave them some order to the endless fun and let the camera crew get the shots they needed.

WHETHER IT WAS WIDE OPEN TUNDRA, THROUGH A FOREST OR OVER AN ABANDONED BRIDGE, IT WAS ALL THE SAME TO THE WOLVES. AS LONG AS THERE WAS SOMEONE WILLING TO LEAD, THE OTHERS WERE ONLY TOO HAPPY TO CHASE.

Days like these were great for everyone. It let them see the wolves were happy and carefree and capable of having fun. One of the crew said watching them play and run free in the fresh snow made him feel as if he was watching an Opera. Since I've never been to the Opera, my guess is it's a great thing to see.

Eat the Legs, Not the Actor!

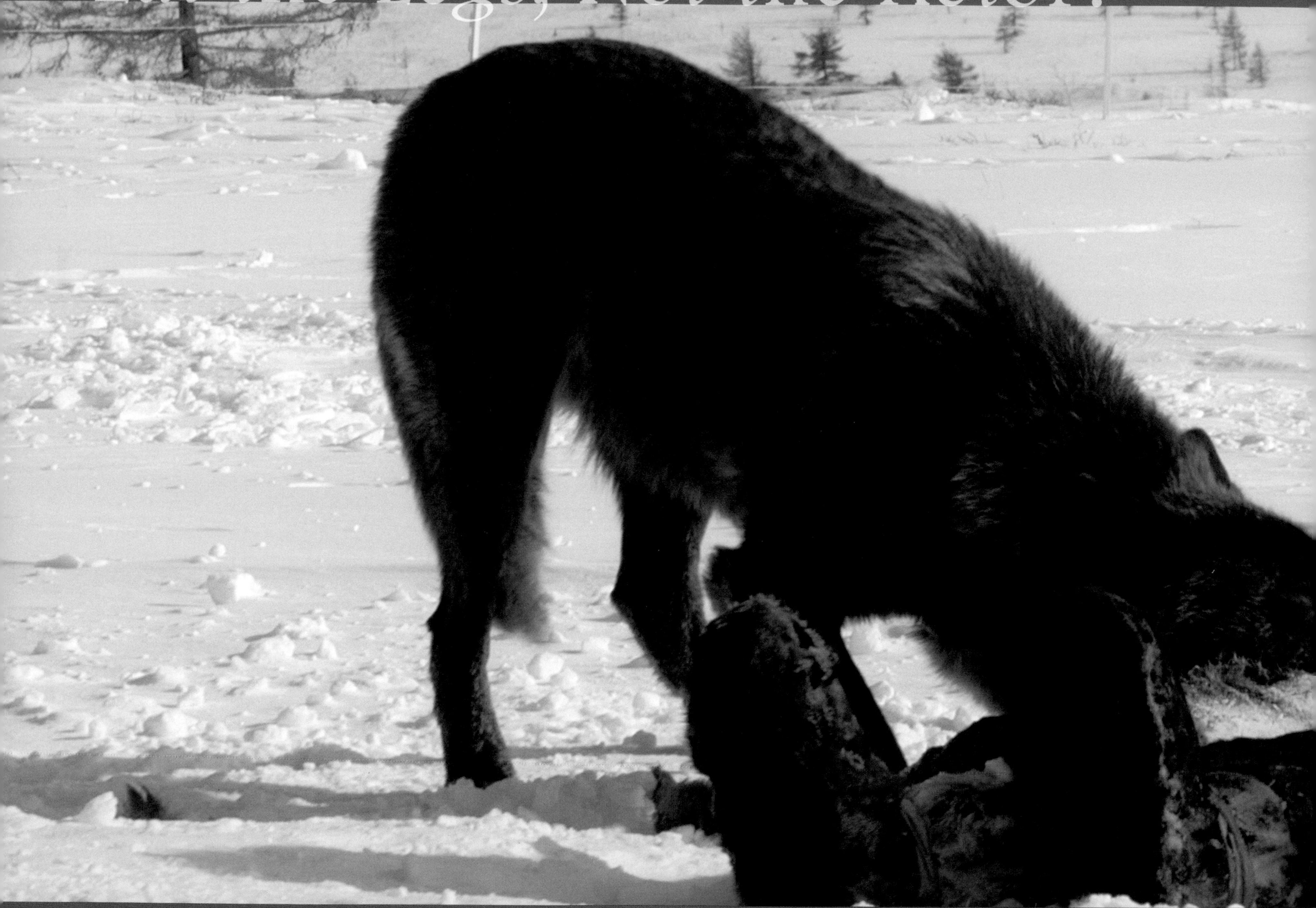

This scene was a true test of the circle of trust between the wolves, the actor and myself. It was one of the most challenging sequences we had during the winter months of filming.

In this dream sequence, the actor is lying in the snow and the wolves come and begin to eat his legs. In order for this to work, his real legs are hidden underneath the frozen ice and fake legs are on top.

Due to the position of the camera, the actor had to keep his eyes closed the entire time the wolves were eating the fake legs. The courage the young actor showed during the filming of this scene was incredible.

INSIDE BOTH FAKE LEGS I HID LARGE BONES WITH MEAT STILL ATTACHED TO THEM. BY CUTTING SMALL HOLES IN THE FUR OF THE FAKE LEGS, THE WOLVES CAN FOCUS ON THIS AREA AND HOPEFULLY FORGET ABOUT THE ACTOR LYING JUST INCHES AWAY.

THIS SCENE REQUIRED THE CAMERA TO START VERY CLOSE TO THE WOLVES AND SLOWLY MOVE UPWARD UNTIL IT WAS DIRECTLY ABOVE THEM. THE WHOLE TIME, THE WOLVES HAD TO KEEP EATING THE FAKE LEGS WITHOUT MOVING AWAY UNTIL THE SCENE WAS OVER.

Wolves are very cautious animals. They are suspicious of everything, especially an object moving over their heads. They kept tremendous focus and ignored their wild instincts during this scene.

We did many difficult scenes with the wolves in Siberia. It seemed the more we did, the more was expected of the wolves. But apart from my crew and myself, I doubt anyone really understood how complicated and difficult this scene was for us to film.

When I first read the script I imagined many of the sequences would be done with the help of computers. Especially the scenes with wolves and reindeer together. Then the decision was made to do it practically... who does that practically?

The wolves had already done several scenes working beside the reindeer and it had all worked out great. But this was going to be a lot different. Now we would be moving at speed, travelling far from the security of the other people if anything should go wrong.

THE ONE ELEMENT I DID NOT KNOW ABOUT WAS THE THIRD REINDEER ATTACHED BEHIND THE SLED. IT WAS IN A VERY VULNERABLE POSITION, OUT OF MY LINE OF SIGHT BUT WELL WITHIN REACH OF A CURIOUS WOLF.

During all the time we spent with the wolves and the reindeer sled, everything went well. However, one day the combination of a nervous reindeer and an overenthusiastic wolf called Digger did cause me some trouble! But that was just a small bump compared to the beautiful images that were filmed in these scenes.

There were many things we did with the wolves on this project that had never been done before. Some things I wasn't sure we could do at all. But the days the wolves ran free following me on the reindeer sled were some of my proudest moments. It was predator and prey working together. It was the heart of the film and it was magical.

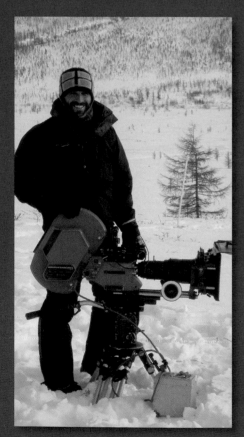

A FILM SET CAN BE A VERY STRANGE AND CONFUSING PLACE FOR A WOLF. NOT ONLY ARE THERE MORE PEOPLE AROUND THAN THEY NORMALLY SEE AT ONE TIME, BUT THERE IS AN ENDLESS AMOUNT OF STRANGE EQUIPMENT ALWAYS POINTED IN THEIR DIRECTION. SOMETIMES THERE CAN BE THREE OR FOUR CAMERAS COVERING A SCENE. NOT ONLY DOES THIS MAKE IT DIFFICULT FOR THE TRAINER TO HIDE, IT MEANS THE WOLF HAS TO GET USED TO BEING SURROUNDED BY THESE STRANGE-LOOKING OBJECTS.

Sometimes when you are on a location scout or in a production meeting, the simple comment is often made that "for this shot we will put the camera on a crane." From a wolf's perspective you may as well say "we'll attach the camera to a monolithic, prehistoric-looking thing that will tower over the trees and look down on you." It's up to us to try and explain to the wolf that it's ok.

A RELATIONSHIP BETWEEN THE CAMERA CREW AND THE TRAINERS AND WOLVES IS SO IMPORTANT IN MAKING AN ANIMAL FILM. NOT ONLY WILL YOU BE SPENDING A LONG TIME TOGETHER, BUT YOU MUST UNDERSTAND HOW EACH OTHER WORKS IN ORDER TO GET THE SHOTS REQUIRED.

Once the wolves get comfortable with the camera crew they will accept them being in very close proximity without feeling nervous or threatened. We always know the relationship is going well when the crew start referring to the wolves by name instead of just "the wolf."

This was the first time I had ever taken a real carcass away from my wolves. Once they were presented with this surprise meal, everything about their behaviour changed. They were no longer just acting film wolves.

TO THEM THIS WAS JUST AS IF THEY HAD MADE A KILL IN THE WILD.

INSTINCT TOOK OVER AND THEY DID NOT WANT TO GIVE IT UP —

EVEN TO ME.

At this moment, it was easy to forget this wolf used to sleep on my bed at home and her name was Sweet Pea!

EVERYWHERE YOU LOOKED WAS SIMPLY AMAZING AND UNTOUCHED. YOU COULD SEE FOR MILES AND THE LANDSCAPE WAS FREE FROM BUILDINGS, POWER POLES AND ALL OTHER SIGNS OF HUMAN LIFE. FROM THE CLEAR BLUE SKIES OF THE FREEZING WINTER, TO THE BREATHTAKING VIEW FROM THE WOLF DEN LOCATION IN SUMMER, THIS TRULY WAS A SPECIAL PLACE.

On our final day of filming, we travelled by helicopter to a distant mountaintop. Once again, the scenery was 360 degrees of pure visual delight for any film crew. A stunning display of nature's beauty — no computer effects needed.

The day we arrived at the farthest filming location, deep in the mountains, we were surprised to find wild wolf tracks disappearing into the distance on the pristine snow. Knowing these wild creatures roam free here, and seeing the fresh tracks, gave us a great feeling that day. This was the most beautiful thing I had seen so far.

All wolves are capable of snarling —
for them, it's just another way of
communicating with other members
of the pack. But not all of them
have the confidence to snarl in
front of a camera. For them it's
typically a triggered display kept
for personal interaction between
wolves, not something to be shown
to the world at a moment's notice.

It's only by spending endless hours raising and training our wolves that we can see which ones have a personality strong enough to demonstrate this behaviour when the camera is rolling. And as you can see in these photos I have chosen, some of them just love to show their teeth!

For me there is nothing as cute as a baby wolf pup. When I found out we needed pups for the Summer shooting, a part of me was excited about tiny little paws tearing through my house again. And no doubt, like any expectant parent, a small part of me could not help but think about all the sleepless nights to come...

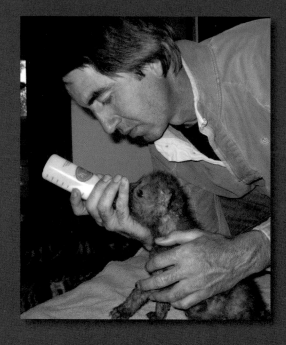

The next few weeks consist of around-the-clock bottle feeding, followed by trying to convince them that solid food is good for them even if it is messier.

As they get past the first puppy weeks, they barely fit on the household scale anymore. I can't wait to see if they will grow as big and strong as we imagine.

Going Fishing: Sometimes when you read a script it's easy to over-think things. Like a scene where a butterfly plays with the small pups near the wolf den. The simple way is to tie a fake plastic butterfly onto a fishing pole and go fishing! This gets the pups looking in the right direction for the camera, and then the plastic butterfly is easily replaced by a computer-generated one in post-production — a perfect example of keeping it simple.

From helpless pups to travelling around the world, they had shown tremendous resilience to everything they had experienced so far in their life. I was so very proud of them.

Most of our summer filming would take place at this one location. It was a truly beautiful place, with breathtaking views in every direction. This was also where the pups would make their first camera appearance.

Once we had put Tyka in her position under the rock and the cameras would roll, we would bring in the pups. Their natural instinct would take over to make the scene come alive. Tyka turned into the super mom she is and the pups were only too happy to climb all over her. But Quigley would always try his hardest to get up on the rock and pretend to be a big wolf.

Sally Jo Sousa

THERE WAS NOTHING EASY ABOUT THIS PROJECT FOR ME. BUT THE
FACT I SUCCEEDED IN GETTING THE WHOLE JOB DONE WAS DUE TO
THE COMMITMENT OF MY TEAM.

Rowan Harland

THEY WERE THE BACKBONE OF THE
PROJECT FOR ME. THEY WERE ALWAYS
THERE WITH SUPPORT, ENERGY
AND ENTHUSIASM THROUGHOUT
THE WHOLE THING.

David Gilchrist

Alexis De Mangelaere

Mike Scriba

And despite the extreme cold or the sweltering heat we always managed to find something to laugh about each day.

Guillaume Mazille

Katherine Engelmann

I would like to take this opportunity to thank them all for everything they did to make my life easier.

Cory Gwyn

Mark Breese

Marie Schneider

Digger

Equally a part of
the team were the
wolves. Without their
unwavering confidence and
trust we would have
achieved nothing in Siberia.
They did more than I
ever expected or could
ever have hoped for.

Tyka

2-Toes

THEY NEVER LET ME DOWN AND THEY
FOUGHT AGAINST THEIR INSTINCTS
MANY TIMES TO GET US THE
FOOTAGE WE NEEDED.

Sweet Pea

Toby

WORDS CANNOT DESCRIBE HOW MUCH
I FEEL TOWARD THEM OR HOW
MUCH I OWE THEM.

Jack

Zinger

Scrunch

Arthur

T-Bone

Quigley

Thunder

Ripley

It's when you put your hand out and they find it, or when you have a thought and they do it before you can ask. It's when you look into their eyes and they look back at you with acknowledgement. And when you can spend hours together without needing anything but the company of each other.

I would tell him I love him, and that he means the world to me. And I would say sorry for everything I put him through.

Dedicated to Josh Hurlburt – Your laughter is missed.

Photo credits

© **David Gilchrist** pages 13, 17,19 (bottom) 21, 22, 25, 26, 27 (bottom) 29, 35, 36 (top x 2), 37, 40 (x2), 41, 42, 43 (x2), 44 (top x2), 52, 56 (top x2, bottom right), 57, 60, 61 (right & bottom left), 65, 66 (x6), 78 (top right, bottom left), 79, 80, 81, 82, 83, 84/85, 87, 88, 89 (top), 90/91, 92, 96 (top & bottom), 98 (x3), 99 (left), 106, 107 (top right/left, bottom middle), 108, 109, 111, 124/125, 126 (top x2), 128 (x2), 130 (x2), 131, 143, 153 (top x2), 160 (x3), 161, 162 (x3), 163, 165, 170 (x3), 171 (top), 178, 179, 186 (left), 187 (x2), 188 (x2), 189 (x3), 190, 191 (left, right top/middle), 193, 195 (right), 196 (x4), 197 (x4), 200/201, 206 (top), 211, 212.

© **Sylvain Bardoux** pages 5, 49, 56 (bottom left), 58 (top, bottom right), 61 (top), 94, 95, 99 (right), 101, 112/113, 116 (top/bottom), 120 (bottom), 127, 140/141, 145, 156/157, 164 (x2), 166/167, 169, 171 (bottom x2), 173, 174 (left), 177, 181, 194 (x2), 195 (left), 203, 206 (bottom), 213.

© **Didier Langou** pages 2, 6, 62/63, 68, 69, 71, 115, 120 (top), 121 (bottom x2), 147, 182/183, 184, 205.

© **Patrick Blin** pages 44 (bottom x2), 45, 46 (top), 47, 74/75, 97, 107 (bottom right/left), 121 (top), 132/133, 135, 136, 137 (x2), 138, 139, 152, 172, 174 (right), 175, 176, 209.

© **Marie Schneider** pages 77, 78 (top left, bottom right), 102/103, 105, 107 (top middle), 129, 148/149, 151, 153 (bottom), 154, 155 (x3), 192, 199 (top), 208.

© **Guillaume Mazille** pages 10, 117, 118 (top/bottom), 119, 123.

© **Alexey Golovinov** pages 38/39, 46 (bottom), 48, 142, 144, 198 (x4), 199 (bottom left/right).

© **Kasia Wandycz** pages 30/31, 32.

© **Andrew Simpson** pages 14/15, 18, 19 (top), 23, 24, 27 (top x2), 50/51, 54, 55 (right), 58 (bottom left), 72, 89 (bottom), 126 (bottom), 185, 186 (right), 191 (bottom right).

© **André Caviller** page 36 (bottom).

© **Stéphane Paillard** page 204.

© **Sally Jo Sousa** pages 55 (left), 59, 158.

Rocky Mountain Books
www.rmbooks.com

Library and Archives Canada Cataloguing in Publication

Simpson, Andrew, 1966–
     Wolves unleashed / Andrew Simpson.

Also issued in electronic format.
ISBN 978-1-927330-18-0 (HTML).—ISBN 978-1-927330-32-6 (PDF)
ISBN 978-1-927330-17-3 (bound)

     1. Wolves. 2. Simpson, Andrew, 1966–. 3. Human-animal relationships.
4. Animal trainers—Canada—Biography. I. Title.

QL737.C22S54 2012   599.773   C2012-903842-3

Book design: Tina Sarantis

Printed in Canada

Rocky Mountain Books acknowledges the financial support for its publishing program from the Government of Canada through the Canada Book Fund (CBF) and the Canada Council for the Arts, and from the province of British Columbia through the British Columbia Arts Council and the Book Publishing Tax Credit.

  Canadian Heritage Patrimoine canadien   Canada Council for the Arts Conseil des Arts du Canada   BRITISH COLUMBIA ARTS COUNCIL
Supported by the Province of British Columbia

This book was produced using FSC®-certified, acid-free paper, processed chlorine free and printed with vegetable-based inks.

 FSC
www.fsc.org

MIX
Paper from
responsible sources
FSC® C016245